CHINESE
HOROSCOPES
FOR
LOVERS

The Rooster

LORI REID

illustrated by
PAUL COLLICUTT

ELEMENT BOOKS

Shaftesbury, Dorset • Rockport, Massachusetts • Brisbane, Queensland

© Lori Reid 1996

First published in Great Britain in 1996 by

ELEMENT BOOKS LIMITED

Shaftesbury, Dorset SP7 8BP

Published in the USA in 1996 by

ELEMENT BOOKS, INC.

PO Box 830, Rockport, MA 01966

Published in Australia in 1996 by

ELEMENT BOOKS LIMITED

for JACARANDA WILEY LIMITED

33 Park Road, Milton, Brisbane 4064

Designed and created by

THE BRIDGEWATER BOOK COMPANY

Art directed by *Peter Bridgewater*

Designed by *Angela Neal*

Picture research by *Vanessa Fletcher*

Edited by *Gillian Delaforce*

Printed and bound in Great Britain by
BPC Paulton Books Ltd

British Library Cataloguing in Publication data available

Library of Congress Cataloging in Publication data available

ISBN 1-85230-770-6

Contents

Why are some people lucky in love and others not?

Chinese Astrology

SOME PEOPLE fall in love and, as the fairy tales go, live happily ever after. Others fall in love – again and again, make the same mistakes every time and never form a lasting relationship. Most of us come between these two extremes, and

some people form remarkably successful unions while others make spectacular disasters of their personal lives. Why are some people lucky in love while others have the odds stacked against them?

ANIMAL NAMES

According to the philosophy of the Far East, luck has very little

to do with it. The answer, the philosophers say, lies with 'the Animal that hides in our hearts'. This Animal, of which there are 12, forms part of the complex art of Chinese Astrology. Each year of a 12-year cycle is attributed an Animal sign, whose characteristics are said to influence worldly events as well as the personality and fate of each living thing that comes under its dominion. The 12 Animals run in sequence, beginning with the Rat and followed by the Ox, Tiger, Rabbit, Dragon, Snake, Horse, Sheep, Monkey, Rooster, Dog and last, but not least, the Pig. Being born in the Year of the Ox, for example, is simply a way of describing what you're like, physically and psychologically. And this is quite different from someone who, for instance, is born in the Year of the Snake.

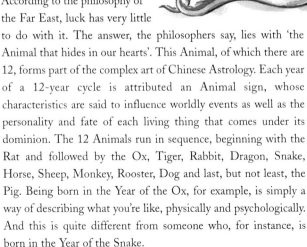

9

*The 12
Animals
of Chinese
Astrology.*

RELATIONSHIPS

These Animal names are merely the tip of the
ice-berg, considering the complexity of the whole
subject. Yet such are the richness and wisdom of Chinese
Astrology that understanding the principles behind the year in
which you were born will give you powerful insights into your
own personality. The system is very specific about which Animals
are compatible and which are antagonistic and this tells us
whether our relationships will be successful. Marriages are made
in heaven, so the saying goes. The heavens, according to Chinese
beliefs, can point the way. The rest is up to us.

10

Year Chart and Birth Dates

UNLIKE THE WESTERN CALENDAR, which is based on the Sun, the Oriental year is based on the movement of the Moon, which means that New Year's Day does not fall on a fixed date. This Year Chart, taken from the Chinese Perpetual Calendar, lists the dates on which each year begins and ends together with its Animal ruler for the year. In addition, the Chinese believe that the tangible world is composed of 5 elements, each slightly adapting the characteristics of the Animal signs. These elemental influences are also given here. Finally, the aspect, that is, whether the year is characteristically Yin (-) or Yang (+), is also listed.

The Western calendar is based on the Sun; the Oriental on the Moon.

YIN AND YANG

Yin and Yang are the terms given to the dynamic complementary forces that keep the universe in balance and which are the central principles behind life. Yin is all that is considered negative, passive, feminine, night, the Moon, while Yang is considered positive, active, masculine, day, the Sun.

Year	From – To	Animal sign	Element	Aspect
1900	31 Jan 1900 – 18 Feb 1901	Rat	Metal	+ Yang
1901	19 Feb 1901 – 7 Feb 1902	Ox	Metal	– Yin
1902	8 Feb 1902 – 28 Jan 1903	Tiger	Water	+ Yang
1903	29 Jan 1903 – 15 Feb 1904	Rabbit	Water	– Yin
1904	16 Feb 1904 – 3 Feb 1905	Dragon	Wood	+ Yang
1905	4 Feb 1905 – 24 Jan 1906	Snake	Wood	– Yin
1906	25 Jan 1906 – 12 Feb 1907	Horse	Fire	+ Yang
1907	13 Feb 1907 – 1 Feb 1908	Sheep	Fire	– Yin
1908	2 Feb 1908 – 21 Jan 1909	Monkey	Earth	+ Yang
1909	22 Jan 1909 – 9 Feb 1910	Rooster	Earth	– Yin
1910	10 Feb 1910 – 29 Jan 1911	Dog	Metal	+ Yang
1911	30 Jan 1911 – 17 Feb 1912	Pig	Metal	– Yin
1912	18 Feb 1912 – 5 Feb 1913	Rat	Water	+ Yang
1913	6 Feb 1913 – 25 Jan 1914	Ox	Water	– Yin
1914	26 Jan 1914 – 13 Feb 1915	Tiger	Wood	+ Yang
1915	14 Feb 1915 – 2 Feb 1916	Rabbit	Wood	– Yin
1916	3 Feb 1916 – 22 Jan 1917	Dragon	Fire	+ Yang
1917	23 Jan 1917 – 10 Feb 1918	Snake	Fire	– Yin
1918	11 Feb 1918 – 31 Jan 1919	Horse	Earth	+ Yang
1919	1 Feb 1919 – 19 Feb 1920	Sheep	Earth	– Yin
1920	20 Feb 1920 – 7 Feb 1921	Monkey	Metal	+ Yang
1921	8 Feb 1921 – 27 Jan 1922	Rooster	Metal	– Yin
1922	28 Jan 1922 – 15 Feb 1923	Dog	Water	+ Yang
1923	16 Feb 1923 – 4 Feb 1924	Pig	Water	– Yin
1924	5 Feb 1924 – 24 Jan 1925	Rat	Wood	+ Yang
1925	25 Jan 1925 – 12 Feb 1926	Ox	Wood	– Yin
1926	13 Feb 1926 – 1 Feb 1927	Tiger	Fire	+ Yang
1927	2 Feb 1927 – 22 Jan 1928	Rabbit	Fire	– Yin
1928	23 Jan 1928 – 9 Feb 1929	Dragon	Earth	+ Yang
1929	10 Feb 1929 – 29 Jan 1930	Snake	Earth	– Yin
1930	30 Jan 1930 – 16 Feb 1931	Horse	Metal	+ Yang
1931	17 Feb 1931 – 5 Feb 1932	Sheep	Metal	– Yin
1932	6 Feb 1932 – 25 Jan 1933	Monkey	Water	+ Yang
1933	26 Jan 1933 – 13 Feb 1934	Rooster	Water	– Yin
1934	14 Feb 1934 – 3 Feb 1935	Dog	Wood	+ Yang
1935	4 Feb 1935 – 23 Jan 1936	Pig	Wood	– Yin

鷄

Year	From – To		Animal sign	Element	Aspect	
1936	24 Jan 1936 – 10 Feb 1937		Rat	Fire	+	Yang
1937	11 Feb 1937 – 30 Jan 1938		Ox	Fire	–	Yin
1938	31 Jan 1938 – 18 Feb 1939		Tiger	Earth	+	Yang
1939	19 Feb 1939 – 7 Feb 1940		Rabbit	Earth	–	Yin
1940	8 Feb 1940 – 26 Jan 1941		Dragon	Metal	+	Yang
1941	27 Jan 1941 – 14 Feb 1942		Snake	Metal	–	Yin
1942	15 Feb 1942 – 4 Feb 1943		Horse	Water	+	Yang
1943	5 Feb 1943 – 24 Jan 1944		Sheep	Water	–	Yin
1944	25 Jan 1944 – 12 Feb 1945		Monkey	Wood	+	Yang
1945	13 Feb 1945 – 1 Feb 1946		Rooster	Wood	–	Yin
1946	2 Feb 1946 – 21 Jan 1947		Dog	Fire	+	Yang
1947	22 Jan 1947 – 9 Feb 1948		Pig	Fire	–	Yin
1948	10 Feb 1948 – 28 Jan 1949		Rat	Earth	+	Yang
1949	29 Jan 1949 – 16 Feb 1950		Ox	Earth	–	Yin
1950	17 Feb 1950 – 5 Feb 1951		Tiger	Metal	+	Yang
1951	6 Feb 1951 – 26 Jan 1952		Rabbit	Metal	–	Yin
1952	27 Jan 1952 – 13 Feb 1953		Dragon	Water	+	Yang
1953	14 Feb 1953 – 2 Feb 1954		Snake	Water	–	Yin
1954	3 Feb 1954 – 23 Jan 1955		Horse	Wood	+	Yang
1955	24 Jan 1955 – 11 Feb 1956		Sheep	Wood	–	Yin
1956	12 Feb 1956 – 30 Jan 1957		Monkey	Fire	+	Yang
1957	31 Jan 1957 – 17 Feb 1958		Rooster	Fire	–	Yin
1958	18 Feb 1958 – 7 Feb 1959		Dog	Earth	+	Yang
1959	8 Feb 1959 – 27 Jan 1960		Pig	Earth	–	Yin
1960	28 Jan 1960 – 14 Feb 1961		Rat	Metal	+	Yang
1961	15 Feb 1961 – 4 Feb 1962		Ox	Metal	–	Yin
1962	5 Feb 1962 – 24 Jan 1963		Tiger	Water	+	Yang
1963	25 Jan 1963 – 12 Feb 1964		Rabbit	Water	–	Yin
1964	13 Feb 1964 – 1 Feb 1965		Dragon	Wood	+	Yang
1965	2 Feb 1965 – 20 Jan 1966		Snake	Wood	–	Yin
1966	21 Jan 1966 – 8 Feb 1967		Horse	Fire	+	Yang
1967	9 Feb 1967 – 29 Jan 1968		Sheep	Fire	–	Yin
1968	30 Jan 1968 – 16 Feb 1969		Monkey	Earth	+	Yang
1969	17 Feb 1969 – 5 Feb 1970		Rooster	Earth	–	Yin
1970	6 Feb 1970 – 26 Jan 1971		Dog	Metal	+	Yang
1971	27 Jan 1971 – 15 Jan 1972		Pig	Metal	–	Yin

13

Year	From – To	Animal sign	Element	Aspect	
1972	16 Jan 1972 – 2 Feb 1973	Rat	Water	+	Yang
1973	3 Feb 1973 – 22 Jan 1974	Ox	Water	–	Yin
1974	23 Jan 1974 – 10 Feb 1975	Tiger	Wood	+	Yang
1975	11 Feb 1975 – 30 Jan 1976	Rabbit	Wood	–	Yin
1976	31 Jan 1976 – 17 Feb 1977	Dragon	Fire	+	Yang
1977	18 Feb 1977 – 6 Feb 1978	Snake	Fire	–	Yin
1978	7 Feb 1978 – 27 Jan 1979	Horse	Earth	+	Yang
1979	28 Jan 1979 – 15 Feb 1980	Sheep	Earth	–	Yin
1980	16 Feb 1980 – 4 Feb 1981	Monkey	Metal	+	Yang
1981	5 Feb 1981 – 24 Jan 1982	Rooster	Metal	–	Yin
1982	25 Jan 1982 – 12 Feb 1983	Dog	Water	+	Yang
1983	13 Feb 1983 – 1 Feb 1984	Pig	Water	–	Yin
1984	2 Feb 1984 – 19 Feb 1985	Rat	Wood	+	Yang
1985	20 Feb 1985 – 8 Feb 1986	Ox	Wood	–	Yin
1986	9 Feb 1986 – 28 Jan 1987	Tiger	Fire	+	Yang
1987	29 Jan 1987 – 16 Feb 1988	Rabbit	Fire	–	Yin
1988	17 Feb 1988 – 5 Feb 1989	Dragon	Earth	+	Yang
1989	6 Feb 1989 – 26 Jan 1990	Snake	Earth	–	Yin
1990	27 Jan 1990 – 14 Feb 1991	Horse	Metal	+	Yang
1991	15 Feb 1991 – 3 Feb 1992	Sheep	Metal	–	Yin
1992	4 Feb 1992 – 22 Jan 1993	Monkey	Water	+	Yang
1993	23 Jan 1993 – 9 Feb 1994	Rooster	Water	–	Yin
1994	10 Feb 1994 – 30 Jan 1995	Dog	Wood	+	Yang
1995	31 Jan 1995 – 18 Feb 1996	Pig	Wood	–	Yin
1996	19 Feb 1996 – 7 Feb 1997	Rat	Fire	+	Yang
1997	8 Feb 1997 – 27 Jan 1998	Ox	Fire	–	Yin
1998	28 Jan 1998 – 15 Feb 1999	Tiger	Earth	+	Yang
1999	16 Feb 1999 – 4 Feb 2000	Rabbit	Earth	–	Yin
2000	5 Feb 2000 – 23 Jan 2001	Dragon	Metal	+	Yang
2001	24 Jan 2001 – 11 Feb 2002	Snake	Metal	–	Yin
2002	12 Feb 2002 – 31 Jan 2003	Horse	Water	+	Yang
2003	1 Feb 2003 – 21 Jan 2004	Sheep	Water	–	Yin
2004	22 Jan 2004 – 8 Feb 2005	Monkey	Wood	+	Yang
2005	9 Feb 2005 – 28 Jan 2006	Rooster	Wood	–	Yin
2006	29 Jan 2006 – 17 Feb 2007	Dog	Fire	+	Yang
2007	18 Feb 2007 – 6 Feb 2008	Pig	Fire	–	Yin

14

Introducing the Animals

| THE RAT | ♥ ♥ ♥ DRAGON, MONKEY | ✖ HORSE |

Outwardly cool, Rats are passionate lovers with depths of feeling that others don't often recognize. Rats are very self-controlled.

| THE OX | ♥ ♥ ♥ SNAKE, ROOSTER | ✖ SHEEP |

Not necessarily the most romantic of the signs, Ox people make steadfast lovers as well as faithful, affectionate partners.

| THE TIGER | ♥ ♥ ♥ HORSE, DOG | ✖ MONKEY |

Passionate and sensual, Tigers are exciting lovers. Flirty when young, once committed they make stable partners and keep their sexual allure.

| THE RABBIT | ♥ ♥ ♥ SHEEP, PIG | ✖ ROOSTER |

Gentle, emotional and sentimental, Rabbits make sensitive lovers. They are shrewd and seek a partner who offers security.

| THE DRAGON | ♥ ♥ ♥ RAT, MONKEY | ✖ DOG |

Dragon folk get as much stimulation from mind-touch as they do through sex. A partner on the same wave-length is essential.

| THE SNAKE | ♥ ♥ ♥ OX, ROOSTER | ✖ PIG |

Deeply passionate, strongly sexed but not aggressive, snakes are attracted to elegant, refined partners. But they are deeply jealous and possessive.

♥ ♥ ♥ *COMPATIBLE* ✖ *INCOMPATIBLE*

15

THE HORSE	♥ ♥ ♥ TIGER, DOG	✖ RAT

For horse-born folk love is blind. In losing their hearts, they lose their heads and make several mistakes before finding the right partner.

THE SHEEP	♥ ♥ ♥ RABBIT, PIG	✖ OX

Sheep-born people are made for marriage. Domesticated home-lovers, they find emotional satisfaction with a partner who provides security.

THE MONKEY	♥ ♥ ♥ DRAGON, RAT	✖ TIGER

Clever and witty, Monkeys need partners who will keep them stimulated. Forget the 9 to 5 routine, these people need *pizzazz*.

THE ROOSTER	♥ ♥ ♥ OX, SNAKE	✖ RABBIT

The Rooster's stylish good looks guarantee they will attract many suitors. They are level-headed and approach relationships coolly.

THE DOG	♥ ♥ ♥ TIGER, HORSE	✖ DRAGON

A loving, stable relationship is an essential component in the lives of Dogs. Once they have found their mate, they remain faithful for life.

THE PIG	♥ ♥ ♥ RABBIT, SHEEP	✖ SNAKE

These are sensual hedonists who enjoy lingering love-making between satin sheets. Caviar and champagne go down very nicely too.

The Rooster Personality

YEARS OF THE ROOSTER

1909 ★ 1921 ★ 1933 ★ 1945 ★ 1957
1969 ★ 1981 ★ 1993 ★ 2005

COLOURFUL AND FLAMBOYANT, being born under the tenth Chinese Animal sign means that you're a feisty individual: tough, resilient, confident and strong-willed. Like the barn-yard creature who represents so many of your characteristics, you're proud, extrovert and theatrical. Indeed, many Rooster-born folk are downright show-offs with a tendency to strut around a good deal. But to give you your due, you're honest and plain-speaking; as far as you're concerned, a spade's a spade.

ROOSTER FACTS

Tenth in order ★ *Chinese name – Ji* ★ *Sign of honesty*
★ *Hour – 5PM – 6.59PM* ★ *Month – September* ★
★ *Western counterpart – Virgo* ★

CHARACTERISTICS

♥ *Resilience* ♥ *Courage* ♥ *Passion* ♥ *Protectiveness*
♥ *Patriotism* ♥ *Industriousness*

✖ *Bluntness* ✖ *Conceit* ✖ *Rudeness* ✖ *Impatience*
✖ *Aggression* ✖ *Bossiness*

鶏

17

At any gathering the Rooster loves to shine and entertain.

LOYAL ROOSTER

You're not given to trickery or underhandedness of any sort. In fact, there's nothing you despise more than deceit and disloyalty; you like to put your cards on the table and respect those who are candid enough to do the same. On the other hand, you can be the life and soul of any social gathering – witty, highly amusing and one of the most entertaining joke-tellers or after-dinner speakers in the neighbourhood.

A PERFECTIONIST

Despite a tendency to melodrama you are immensely practical and logical. Perhaps one of the most hard-working of the signs, you possess excellent powers of discrimination and are a stickler for detail. With such high standards of excellence you can be, in short, a perfectionist.

Roosters have a fiercely keen eye for the detail and minutiae of life.

Your Hour of Birth

WHILE YOUR YEAR OF BIRTH describes your fundamental character, the Animal governing the actual hour in which you were born describes your outer temperament, how people see you or the picture you present to the outside world. Note that each Animal rules over two consecutive hours. Also note that these are GMT standard times and that adjustments need to be made if you were born during Summer or daylight saving time.

11PM – 12.59AM ★ RAT

Pleasant, sociable, easy to get on with. An active, confident, busy person – and a bit of a busybody to boot.

1AM – 2.59AM ★ OX

Level-headed and down-to-earth, you come across as knowledgeable and reliable – sometimes, though, a bit biased.

3AM – 4.59AM ★ TIGER

Enthusiastic and self-assured, people see you as a strong and positive personality – at times a little over-exuberant.

5AM – 6.59AM ★ RABBIT

You're sensitive and shy and don't project your real self to the world. You feel you have to put on an act to please others.

7AM – 8.59AM ★ DRAGON

Independent and interesting, you present a picture of someone who is quite out of the ordinary.

9AM – 10.59AM ★ SNAKE

You can be a bit difficult to fathom and, because you appear so controlled, people either take to you instantly, or not at all.

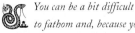

 11AM – 12.59PM ★ HORSE
Open, cheerful and happy-go-lucky is the picture you always put across to others. You're an extrovert and it generally shows.

 5PM – 6.59PM ★ ROOSTER
There's something rather stylish in your approach that gives people an impression of elegance and glamour. But you don't suffer fools gladly.

19

 1PM – 2.59PM ★ SHEEP
Your unassuming nature won't allow you to foist yourself upon others so people see you as quiet and retiring – but eminently sensible, though.

 7PM – 8.59PM ★ DOG
Some people see you as steady and reliable, others as quiet and graceful and others still as dull and unimaginative. It all depends who you're with at the time.

 3PM – 4.59PM ★ MONKEY
Lively and talkative, that twinkle in your eye will guarantee you make friends wherever you go.

 9PM – 10.59PM ★ PIG
Your laid-back manner conceals a depth of interest and intelligence that doesn't always come through at first glance.

Your hour of birth describes your outer temperament.

20

The Rooster Lover

A person who is ready to stand by you through thick and thin will find in you a partner who is an excellent provider, caring, loving, devoted, steadfast and loyal as the live-long day.

WHERE ROOSTERS ARE CONCERNED, emotions tend to be black or white, so you either love or hate – with very little room for any grey areas. Yours is a strong, forceful personality and although as a rule candid and open in all your interactions with others, you tend to keep your emotions firmly under wraps and are reluctant to talk about your innermost feelings. Discretion is definitely the better part of valour for you, and your partners can take comfort in the knowledge that you would never disclose the minutest detail of your intimate sexual exploits.

Roosters know how to wear the mask of discretion and hide their innermost secrets.

HEART OF GOLD

It would be fair to say that you're not the easiest person to live with. And yet, anyone who is prepared to look beyond your bossy, abrasive exterior will find someone who desperately wants to love and be loved, who is anxious to please and is genuinely kind and generous. For, though tough and uncompromising, a Rooster's heart is made of solid gold.

21

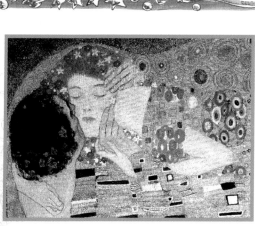

The Kiss
GUSTAV KLIMT 1862–1918

THE PLAIN SPEAKER

It is your very candour, a virtue prized by Roosters, that can actually damage your relationships, especially if your partner tends towards a sensitive disposition.

Never one for mincing your words, you can be highly critical, tactlessly nit-picking and carping about other people's shortcomings. Not only that, but you do have a habit of taking the high moral ground with a sanctimonious smugness that would drive all but the meekest saint straight to the nearest divorce courts.

The Rooster's crowing can drown out friends and family.

22

In Your Element

ALTHOUGH YOUR SIGN recurs every 12 years, each generation is slightly modified by one of 5 elements. If you were born under the Metal influence your character, emotions and behaviour would show significant variations from an individual born under one of the other elements. Check the Year Chart for your ruling element and discover what effects it has upon you.

THE METAL ROOSTER ★ 1921 AND 1981

At times arrogant and highly opinionated, people would describe you as someone who is cocksure. And yet despite your tough self-righteousness, you passionately work to improve the lot of mankind. Learning to compromise would help your relationships.

THE WATER ROOSTER ★ 1933 AND 1993

Generally more intellectual than most other Roosters, you're reasonable and compliant and excel in the world of science and communications. Make an effort to maintain your wide vista throughout your life otherwise your punctilious attention to detail could narrow your field of vision.

THE WOOD ROOSTER ✳ 1945 AND 2005

Kind and considerate, you possess a strong social conscience that drives you to work for the betterment of society. With your boundless energy and enthusiasm, you often take on more than you can realistically handle.

THE FIRE ROOSTER ✳ 1957

Because image is so important to you, you really do spend a lot of time preening your fine feathers. With your dynamic élan you're prone to high theatricals. A brilliant organizer, you make a superb leader or manager in any field in which you choose to use your considerable talents.

THE EARTH ROOSTER ✳ 1909 AND 1969

Careful, methodical, neat and tidy, you're mega-efficient. Never afraid to commit yourself or to take on responsibility, you work hard and expect others to do the same. With your exacting standards and drive to achieve, you have the potential to become highly successful in life.

Partners in Love

THE CHINESE are very definite about which animals are compatible with each other and which are antagonistic. So find out if you're truly suited to your partner.

ROOSTER + RAT
★ *Alas, there's more scratchy conflict than there is tender love between Rats and Roosters.*

ROOSTER + OX
★ *Sexy. Passionate. Sizzling. Top marks for a happy and successful relationship.*

ROOSTER + RABBIT
★ *You're opposites in almost every aspect you could think of.*

ROOSTER + DRAGON
★ *You're exquisite creatures and make a gorgeous pair, but each of you has a mega-ego and that tends to get in the way.*

There are no half measures in the Rooster's love-life.

ROOSTER + TIGER
★ *Misunderstandings between you two strong-minded animals will create problems. Talking about things will help.*

ROOSTER + SNAKE
★ *What a winning team!*

ROOSTER + HORSE
★ *Despite the odd power conflict, you really do make a great couple.*

LOVE PARTNERS AT A GLANCE

Rooster with:	Tips on Togetherness	Compatibility
Rat	too many differences	♥
Ox	blessed by the gods	♥♥♥♥
Tiger	talk or walk	♥♥
Rabbit	nothing in common at all	♥
Dragon	never a dull moment	♥♥
Snake	solid!	♥♥♥♥
Horse	quarrels undermine your love	♥♥♥
Sheep	touch and go	♥
Monkey	soooo picky	♥
Rooster	a disastrous combination	♥
Dog	difficult	♥♥
Pig	worth preserving	♥♥♥

COMPATIBILITY RATINGS:
♥ *conflict* ♥♥ *work at it* ♥♥♥ *strong sexual attraction* ♥♥♥♥ *heavenly!*

鶏

25

ROOSTER + SHEEP
★ *Difficulties at every turn give only average ratings for this union.*

ROOSTER + MONKEY
★ *Romantically, this could be a bit of a damp squib.*

ROOSTER + ROOSTER
★ *So much self-righteousness in one house can only lead to misery.*

ROOSTER + DOG
★ *Not a lot in common here.*

ROOSTER + PIG
★ *Despite your differences, you two could really make a go of this.*

Eiaha ohipa
PAUL GAUGUIN 1848–1903

Rencontre du Soir (detail)
THEOPHILE-
ALEXANDRE
STEINLEN
1859–1923

26

Hot Dates

IF YOU'RE DATING someone for the first time, taking your partner out for a special occasion or simply wanting to re-ignite that flame of passion between you, it helps to understand what would please that person most.

RATS ★ *Wine and dine him or take her to a party. Do something on impulse... go to the races or take a flight in a hot air balloon.*

OXEN ★ *Go for a drive in the country and drop in on a stately home. Visit an art gallery or antique shops. Then have an intimate dinner à deux.*

So glad to see you...
COCA-COLA 1945

TIGERS ★ *Tigers thrive on excitement so go clay-pigeon shooting, Formula One racing or challenge each other to a Quasar dual. A date at the theatre will put stars in your Tiger's eyes.*

RABBITS ★ *Gentle and creative, your Rabbit date will enjoy an evening at home with some take-away food and a romantic video. Play some seductive jazz and snuggle up.*

DRAGONS ★ *Mystery and magic will thrill your Dragon date. Take in a son et lumière show or go to a carnival. Or drive to the coast and sink your toes in the sand as the sun sets.*

SNAKES ★ *Don't do anything too active – these creatures like to take life slooooowly. Hire a row-boat for a long, lazy ride down the river. Give a soothing massage, then glide into a sensual jacuzzi together.*

27

The Carnival
GASTON-DOIN 19/20TH CENTURY

HORSES ★ *Your zany Horse gets easily bored. Take her on a mind-spinning tour of the local attractions. Surprise him with tickets to a musical show. Whatever you do, keep them guessing.*

SHEEP ★ *These folk adore the Arts so visit a museum, gallery or poetry recital. Go to a concert, the ballet, or the opera.*

MONKEYS ★ *The fantastical appeals to this partner, so go to a fancy-dress party or a masked ball, a laser light show or a sci-fi movie.*

ROOSTERS ★ *Grand gestures will impress your Rooster. Escort her to a film première or him to a formal engagement. Dressing up will place this date in seventh heaven.*

DOGS ★ *A cosy dinner will please this most unassuming of partners more than any social occasion. Chatting and story telling will ensure a close understanding.*

PIGS ★ *Arrange a slap-up meal or a lively party, or cruise through the shopping mall. Shopping is one of this partner's favourite hobbies!*

28

Detail from
Chinese
Marriage
Ceremony
CHINESE
PAINTING

Year of Commitment

CAN THE YEAR in which you marry (or make a firm commitment to live together) have any influence upon your marital relationship or the life you and your partner forge together? According to the Orientals, it certainly can. Whether your marriage is fiery, gentle, productive, passionate, insular or sociable doesn't so much depend on your animal nature, as on the nature of the Animal in whose year you tied the knot.

IF YOU MARRY IN A YEAR OF THE...

RAT ★ *your marriage should succeed because ventures starting now attract long-term success. Materially, you won't want and life is full of friendship.*

Marriage Feast
CHINESE PAINTING

OX ★ *your relationship will be solid and tastes conventional. Diligence will be recognized and you'll be well respected.*

TIGER ★ *you'll need plenty of humour to ride out the storms. Marrying in the Year of the Tiger is not auspicious.*

RABBIT ★ *you're wedded under the emblem of lovers. It's auspicious for a happy, carefree relationship, as neither partner wants to rock the boat.*

DRAGON ★ *you're blessed. This year is highly auspicious for luck, happiness and success.*

SNAKE ★ it's good for romance but sexual entanglements are rife. Your relationship may seem languid, but passions run deep.

HORSE ★ chances are you decided to marry on the spur of the moment as the Horse year encourages impetuous behaviour. Marriage now may be volatile.

SHEEP ★ your family and home are blessed but watch domestic spending. Money is very easily frittered away.

Marriage Ceremony
CHINESE PAINTING

MONKEY ★ married life could be unconventional. As plans go awry your lives could be full of surprises.

ROOSTER ★ drama characterizes your married life. Your household will run like clockwork, but bickering could strain your relationship.

DOG ★ it's a truly fortunate year and you can expect domestic joy. Prepare for a large family as the Dog is the sign of fertility!

PIG ★ it's highly auspicious and there'll be plenty of fun. Watch out for indulgence and excess.

Marriage Ceremony (detail)
CHINESE PAINTING

*Detail from
Chinese
Marriage
Ceremony*
CHINESE
PAINTING

TYPICAL ROOSTER PLEASURES

COLOUR PREFERENCES ★ *Peach, apricot*

Topaz   Diamond   Ruby

GEMS AND STONES ★ *Diamond, ruby, topaz*

SUITABLE GIFTS ★ *Brocade waistcoat, egg decorating kit, Bonsai tree, garden trug, terrarium, silver hip flask, ebony walking cane*

HOBBIES AND PASTIMES ★ *Golf, fishing, dressmaking, singing, gardening, making silk flowers, rambling*

Uluru, a Rooster paradise

HOLIDAY PREFERENCES ★ *Nature is a passion so tucking yourself away in the middle of nowhere would be a dream holiday for you. You could walk the fells or lie on your back and conjure images from the clouds in the sky.*

COUNTRIES LINKED WITH THE ROOSTER ★ *Australia, England, West Indies.*

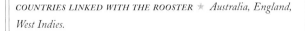

The Rooster Parent

THINK OF A brooding hen clucking over her chicks, picking
and pecking and tucking them under her wings. In just the same
way, you as a Rooster parent nurture and nourish, protect and care
for your youngsters and do all you can to keep your offspring safe
and free from any harm. Such zealous protectiveness, however,
can at times go too far when your natural instincts incline you to
wrap your children from head to toe in cotton wool.

DISCIPLINE

You tend to be strict; most Roosters believe in discipline.
Because you're a stickler for old-fashioned values you bring up
your children to be polite and respectful not only towards their
elders but also to the environment.

> ### THE ROOSTER HABITAT
> *You tend to be houseproud. With your organizational skills your*
> *home is neat and clean; there's a place for everything and everything*
> *is in its place. Hygiene is close to the Rooster's heart and cleansing*
> *agents are tell-tale signs of your Chinese Animal birthright. Your*
> *habit of forever sorting and rearranging, clearing out drawers and*
> *moving furniture around either confuses your long-suffering family or*
> *drives them completely round the bend. Apricots and peaches are the*
> *colours associated with your sign and these blend well with your choice*
> *of classical furniture and traditional décor.*

THE
ROOSTER
PARENT

31

Rooster
parents keep
their chicks
tucked firmly
under their
wings.

32

Animal Babies

FOR SOME parents, their children's personalities harmonize perfectly with their own. Others find that no matter how much they may love their offspring they're just not on the same wave-length. Our children arrive with their characters already well formed and, according to Chinese philosophy, shaped by the influence of their Animal Year. So you should be mindful of the year in which you conceive.

BABIES BORN IN THE YEAR OF THE...

RAT ★ *love being cuddled. They keep on the go – so give them plenty of rest. Later they enjoy collecting things.*

OX ★ *are placid, solid and independent. If not left to their own devices they sulk.*

TIGER ★ *are happy and endearing. As children, they have irrepressible energy. Boys are sporty and girls tom-boys.*

RABBIT ★ *are sensitive and strongly bonded to their mother. They need stability to thrive.*

DRAGON ★ *are independent and imaginative from the start. Encourage any interest that will allow their talents to flourish.*

SNAKE ★ *have great charm. They are slow starters so may need help with school work. Teach them to express feelings.*

鶏

One Hundred Children Scroll
ANON, MING PERIOD

HORSE ★ *will burble away contentedly for hours. Talking starts early and they excel in languages.*

SHEEP ★ *are placid, well-behaved and respectful. They are family-oriented and never stray too far from home.*

MONKEY ★ *take an insatiable interest in everything. With agile minds they're quick to learn. They're good-humoured but mischievous!*

ROOSTER ★ *are sociable. Bright and vivacious, their strong adventurous streak best shows itself on a sports field.*

DOG ★ *are cute and cuddly. Easily pleased, they are content just pottering around the house amusing themselves for hours. Common sense is their greatest virtue.*

PIG ★ *are affectionate and friendly. Well-balanced, self-confident children, they're happy-go-lucky and laid-back. They are popular with friends.*

34

*Roosters are
single
minded in
the hunt for
success.*

Health, Wealth and Worldly Affairs

INVOLVEMENT IN SPORTS and a fondness for the outdoors keep you fit; besides, you're a fighter and won't let ill-health get the better of you. If you do succumb, your excellent recuperative powers soon have you bouncing up and brimming with vitality again. It's in the psychological realm that you're likely to suffer. Prone to dramatic mood swings and driven by exacting standards, it's stress and a tendency to over-indulge that you need to watch.

CAREER

More career-oriented than most other Animals, you're hard-working, status-conscious and driven by ambition. You're suited to a wide variety of occupations, and with determination and indomitable resilience you stick at whatever task you undertake until you have reached your desired goal. No wonder you're such a success and quickly climb the ladder to the top of your chosen profession.

*Roosters are adept at
financial wizardry and
excel in the banking
world. Shrewd, super-
efficient and brilliant at
strategy, it's your natural
talent for organization
that often brings
recognition.*

A love of pomp and pageantry, together with a penchant for donning colourful uniforms and sparkling decorations, often draws Rooster-born folk to the armed forces. Equally, with your humanitarian ideals and highly developed social conscience, many natives of your sign may be found working for charitable organizations.

FINANCES

You're brilliant in any career dealing with money, but when it comes to your own purse-strings, you fall into one of two categories. Either you belong to the band of big-hearted Cockerels who love spending money and showering their friends with gifts or you put it all into a bank and gleefully watch it grow.

FRIENDSHIPS

You tend to have more acquaintances than close friends as you're secretive about your personal life and only allow a few individuals into your inner sanctum. To those you love you're generous but since you're so tactless they need to be thick-skinned!

> ## ROOSTERS MAKE EXCELLENT:
> * Actors * Musicians * Opera singers * Couturiers *
> * Dancers * Armed forces personnel * Secretaries *
> * Dentists * Town councillors * Insurance agents *
> * Dieticians * Book-keepers * Financial advisers *

36

East Meets West

COMBINE YOUR Oriental Animal sign with your Western Zodiac birth sign to form a deeper and richer understanding of your character and personality.

ARIES ROOSTER

★ *Clever, witty and blunt, you expect others to be as honest as yourself. The problem is that some people aren't and you're idealistic enough to believe them just the same.*

TAUREAN ROOSTER

★ *You're industrious to the point of being a workaholic. Learning to relax would help you to lighten your serious outlook. A fun-loving partner would help too.*

GEMINI ROOSTER

★ *Restless and impulsive, you're full of ideas. You admire strength and intelligence and seek a partner with whom you have mind touch. Friends are important to you as is a high-profile social life.*

CANCERIAN ROOSTER

★ *Strongly family-oriented, the more children, pets and other relatives you can gather around you, the happier you feel. Given a loving partner, you'll be faithful, supportive and happy.*

LEONINE ROOSTER

★ *Colourful and flamboyant, you can fill a room with your personality. You're prone to mood-swings and need a reassuring partner to help keep you stable.*

VIRGO ROOSTER

★ *More practical than most Roosters, you excel in tasks that require a logical mentality. A perfectionist, you are apt to drive partners to distraction with your exacting standards.*

鶏

LIBRAN ROOSTER

★ You take an intellectual approach to life. You do not appreciate anything down-market and hate getting yourself messed up – physically or emotionally. Lots of friends and happy companionship are important to you.

SCORPIO ROOSTER

★ The word 'compromise' doesn't exist for you. Strong will and determination mean that when you set your sights on something or someone, you won't give up until you achieve your objective. Emotionally, you're deep to the point of obsession.

SAGITTARIAN ROOSTER

★ It's scrupulous honesty that you look for in a relationship and so even the merest hint of deceit will be enough for you to lose faith in a partner. But you can be both idealistic and altruistic and if someone is in trouble you will never turn your back on them.

CAPRICORN ROOSTER

★ Ambition and worldly aspirations drive you to climb that ladder of success. Efficient and unflappable, it doesn't take long for your superiors to recognize your worth. However, you find it hard to express your feelings.

AQUARIAN ROOSTER

★ You like to stand out, to be different, individualistic or even eccentric. Intellectually, you're streets ahead of everyone else, but you can't bear to be tied down. With a low boredom threshold, you seek fresh challenges to stimulate your imagination.

PISCEAN ROOSTER

★ You're a paradoxical mixture of hard-headed pragmatist and sensitive romantic. Disagreements upset you and you're inclined to look at the world through rose-coloured spectacles. You have a tendency to bend reality a little to fit your idealistic picture of life.

鶏

38

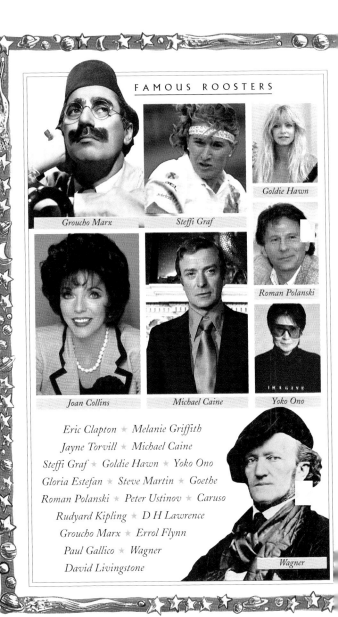

FAMOUS ROOSTERS

Groucho Marx

Steffi Graf

Goldie Hawn

Roman Polanski

Joan Collins

Michael Caine

Yoko Ono

Eric Clapton ★ Melanie Griffith
Jayne Torvill ★ Michael Caine
Steffi Graf ★ Goldie Hawn ★ Yoko Ono
Gloria Estefan ★ Steve Martin ★ Goethe
Roman Polanski ★ Peter Ustinov ★ Caruso
Rudyard Kipling ★ D H Lawrence
Groucho Marx ★ Errol Flynn
Paul Gallico ★ Wagner
David Livingstone

Wagner

The Rooster Year in Focus

鶏

THIS YEAR, IMAGE is all-important. Just as the young cockerel displays fine, colourful plumage so in Rooster years clothes and jewellery hit the headlines. The message to all is: 'If you've got it, flaunt it.'

STICKY RELATIONSHIPS

Relationships are never well-starred in Rooster years; for those having difficulties with their partners reconciliation may not come so easily. The best thing is to steer clear of disagreements and to wait for more harmonious trends next year. We should all beware of nit-picking and of being over-critical.

DOWN WITH BULLIES

This is a time for looking upwards and outwards. Politically and domestically, the down-trodden make their voices heard; the aggrieved or tyrannized will stand up for themselves, and bullies will get their come-uppance.

ACTIVITIES ASSOCIATED
WITH THE ROOSTER YEAR

The discovery, invention, patenting, marketing, manufacturing, formation or first occasion of:
newsreels, insulin, the IMF, the United Nations, interferon, nuclear fusion, man-made satellites.

40

Your Rooster Fortunes
for the Next 12 Years

1996 MARKS THE BEGINNING of a new 12-year cycle in the Chinese calendar. How your relationships and worldly prospects fare will depend on the influence of each Animal year in turn.

1996 YEAR OF THE RAT   *19 Feb 1996 – 6 Feb 1997*

Rat years are never easy for you so 1996 is likely to present you with a few hurdles. Career progress is slow and patchy and heavy expenses may have you dipping into your hard-earned reserves. Relationships, too, create difficulties.

YEAR TREND: KEEP A LOW PROFILE

1997 YEAR OF THE OX   *7 Feb 1997 – 27 Jan 1998*

An auspicious period in which you can recoup last year's losses. At work you make progress, your endeavours reaping their just rewards. Your prestige and reputation increase. Emotional ties bring joy.

YEAR TREND: EXPECT OPENINGS AND OPPORTUNITIES

1998 YEAR OF THE TIGER   *28 Jan 1998 – 15 Feb 1999*

Events happen thick and fast in Tiger years and require quick wits and lightning decisions. Keep on top of the action and you'll come out winning in 1998. Now's the time to set plans in motion and consider your long-term ambitions.

YEAR TREND: COMMITMENT BRINGS SATISFACTION

41

1999 YEAR OF THE RABBIT — *16 Feb 1999 – 4 Feb 2000*

Rabbit years encourage you to overspend so that by the end of the decade you could find yourself seriously out of pocket. Moderating your outlook and expectations minimizes disappointment.

YEAR TREND: **TEAMWORK BRINGS RESULTS**

2000 YEAR OF THE DRAGON — *5 Feb 2000 – 23 Jan 2001*

This is a high spot in the 12-year cycle, when you are given the opportunity to shine. Favourable aspects now encourage you to make great advances which bring prosperity and recognition. Intimate partnerships blossom.

YEAR TREND: **LET YOUR HAIR DOWN**

In the Year of the Snake, the artistic Rooster will blossom.

2001 YEAR OF THE SNAKE — *24 Jan 2001 – 11 Feb 2002*

Last year's favourable auspices sweep you along through the Year of the Snake. Good fortune particularly smiles on those involved in the Arts, the world of music, fashion or anything to do with the beauty industry. Passion sizzles.

YEAR TREND: **PROGRESSIVE**

42

2002 YEAR OF THE HORSE *12 Feb 2002 – 31 Jan 2003*

Typical of the nature of the Horse this will be an erratic year for you although the pluses will balance out the minuses. Romantic liaisons and family life all suffer from the same volatile influences.

YEAR TREND: MIXED FORTUNES

2003 YEAR OF THE SHEEP *1 Feb 2003 – 21 Jan 2004*

A promising year in which you can bring many projects to fruition, advance your worldly expectations and see some very satisfying results to your endeavours. Relax with your loved ones but get out and about to extend your social network.

YEAR TREND: PLEASING DEVELOPMENTS

2004 YEAR OF THE MONKEY *22 Jan 2004 – 8 Feb 2005*

Though opportunities abound for career advancement, problems on the home front will need careful handling this year. Single Rooster-born folk will fare a good deal better than their married counterparts as personal relationships blossom.

YEAR TREND: KEEP AN EYE BEHIND THE SCENES

Roosters can bang the gong for success in their own year.

2005 YEAR OF THE ROOSTER 9 Feb 2005 – 28 Jan 2006

Hooray, this is your year! Because it's your sign it means you will feel confident and relaxed under the Rooster auspices. Now you can further existing plans and projects at work, although new ventures should be put on hold. Domestic affairs bring rewards.

YEAR TREND: **BELIEVE IN YOURSELF**

2006 YEAR OF THE DOG *29 Jan 2006 – 17 Feb 2007*

This is a year for getting your shoulder to the wheel if you want success. Unprofessional conduct and poor workmanship are likely to backfire. Talking through problems could save your relationship.

YEAR TREND: **DON'T TAKE RISKS**

2007 YEAR OF THE PIG *18 Feb 2007 – 6 Feb 2008*

After last year's frustrating slog, the Year of the Pig brings distinct improvement to both career matters and domestic affairs. With romantic ties strengthening and relationships flourishing, the prospects bode well for weddings and new births.

YEAR TREND: **FINANCIAL PRESSURES EASE**